Raven: Scripting Java™ Builds with Ruby

MATTHIEU RIOU

firstPress™

Raven: Scripting Java™ Builds with Ruby

Copyright © 2007 by Matthieu Riou

ISBN-13 (pbk): 978-1-59059-875-7

ISBN-10 (pbk): 1-59059-875-X

Printed and bound in the United States of America (POD)

Lead Editor: Steve Anglin

Technical Reviewer: Matthew Foemmel

Editorial Board: Steve Anglin, Ewan Buckingham, Gary Cornell, Jason Gilmore, Jonathan Gennick, Jonathan Hassell, James Huddleston, Chris Mills, Matthew Moodie, Jeff Pepper, Paul Sarknas, Dominic Shakeshaft, Jim Sumser, Matt Wade

Project Manager: Sofia Marchant

Copy Edit Manager: Nicole Flores

Copy Editor: Marilyn Smith

Assistant Production Director: Kari Brooks-Copony

Compositor: Richard Ables

Cover Designer: Kurt Krames

Manufacturing Director: Tom Debolski

Distributed to the book trade worldwide by Springer-Verlag New York, Inc., 233 Spring Street, 6th Floor, New York, NY 10013. Phone 1-800-SPRINGER, fax 201-348-4505, e-mail orders-ny@springer-sbm.com, or visit http://www.springeronline.com.

For information on translations, please contact Apress directly at 2855 Telegraph Avenue, Suite 600, Berkeley, CA 94705. Phone 510-549-5930, fax 510-549-5939, e-mail info@apress.com, or visit http://www.apress.com.

The source code for this book is available to readers at http://www.apress.com in the Source Code/Download section.

Contents

About the Author

MATTHIEU RIOU has developed software for vendors and also as a freelance consultant, mostly for banks and financial institutions. His technological expertise is centered on Java and J2EE, with a strong web services tint.

Matthieu has also been working on several open source projects and has founded Twister, a Web Services Business Process Execution Language (WS-BPEL) orchestration engine. Since its creation, the orchestration engine project has been donated to the Apache Software Foundation and renamed Apache ODE. Matthieu is still actively contributing on ODE, thanks to his current employer, Intalio, Inc. Additionally, he teaches a few classes for a French university, the *Conservatoire National des Arts et Metiers*.

Matthieu has been enamored with the Ruby language for several years. Raven is his first attempt to bring this love to the open source world.

In his free time, Matthieu enjoys playing guitar and surfing on the California waves. After having deeply loved Paris for several years, he is now enjoying San Francisco just as much.

About the Technical Reviewer

MATTHEW FOEMMEL is a software architect at Business Logic Corporation, based in Chicago, Illinois. He can be reached at foemmelm@businesslogic.com.

Introduction

In this book, we're not going to change the world or solve any fundamentally complex problem. There won't be any transactional or concurrency issues requiring several minutes (or sometimes hours) of deep thoughts. Building a Java project is an accumulation of trivial issues. There's nothing mysterious about it. But as often, the devil is in the details, and there are a lot of details to address when creating a build system.

I've worked on and have seen countless projects where tremendous amounts of time were spent working on the build. Why?

Let's see what building a Java project is about:

* Compiling classes using `javac`

* Building a JAR file to run your program or reuse it in another project

* Managing the project dependencies to produce a compile classpath and try to help as much as possible with the runtime classpath

* Integrating other external tools to run programs like Javadoc, JUnit, XDoclet, and so on

And that's pretty much it. Did you see anything hard to do in this list? I didn't. So why are the solutions you find (mostly the two usual suspects: Apache Ant and Apache Maven) so time-consuming? I've seen people banging their heads against the walls from frustration, and I've often been very close myself to verifying how flat my forehead could be made.

There are multiple answers to this question. A part of it is the overuse of XML, whereas build scripts (as the name says) are supposed to be about scripting. Yes, Ant includes some control statements, but that doesn't make it a full-blown dynamic language. It has been designed as a purely declarative language, and control structures have been added afterward-a bit like a hack. And because it has XML all over the place, it's so verbose! The syntax is just not quite optimal (I'm also thinking of Maven Project Object Models, or POMs, here).

Another part of the answer is dogma-forcing you into certain practices that don't fit your own project. For example, with Maven, there's only one artifact produced per module, and the way around this practice is pretty painful. So if you have single file used by two modules, what do you do? Make a module with it. These theories about how things *should* be done just make it harder for you to write simple builds.

There are actually many more reasons, but my goal here isn't to whine about these or emphasize the shortcomings of other tools. My goal is to show you how simple problems can be solved simply. Raven was born out of my frustration with build problems. I started asking myself, "How would I like my build system to be?" I first selected a powerful scripting language: Ruby. Then I've looked at the simple and efficient tools that already exist in Ruby in the build and dependency management space (RubyGems and Raven). And I started developing.

In this book, you will learn what I came up with. You will discover how Raven is built and how to best use it. My hope is that I have been focused enough in that work and have kept Raven as simple as could be.

CHAPTER 1

Dreams of Build

I know how men in exile feed on dreams of hope.

Aeschylus

First, let's step back a little. I know that we didn't even start yet, so there's nowhere to step back from. But I have the feeling that you are a little too eager to dive into the nitty-gritty details of Raven. It's a wonderful piece of software (and I'm as impartial as can be), but before showing you what Raven is, I would like to talk about what it *should* be. It's always good to dream for a while and build an ideal picture of how you would like things to be. Then when you're face to face with reality, you can immediately see what's wrong, criticize it knowingly, and even improve it.

However, there's a little problem here, and I know you've spotted it already. How could I know about your dream and see what your ideal picture of a build system is? How could I know what would be your best and easiest way to declare the compilation of Java classes? Sadly, I can't. And this might be hard to work around. Plus, we have no time to lose; we have bigger fish to fry. So I'll ask you to trust me and believe in my dream. This is a lot to ask, as we're not even in the third paragraph yet. But if you follow my lead, I'll do my best not to disappoint you.

The First Acronym: DSL

I had a dream (does that sound familiar?) of a build system that would be both simple and flexible—one that would allow me to perform simple tasks quickly, without making fancier tasks close to impossible. But let's start from the beginning. The base commands should be as follows:

build compile -> compiles your Java classes and places the class files close by
build jar -> creates a JAR file using your classes

Nearly every Java project will need this. But every project also has its specific requirements. So we'll need to do other things as well, like this:

build publish_site -> publishes the project web site to a public server
build jar_interfaces -> creates another JAR containing only public interfaces

Here, I've just illustrated the notion of a *task*. It's simply a self-contained operation that can be called from the command line. But tasks can also depend on each other. For example, the jar task can automatically call the compile task. It just makes everything easier.

So far, so good. There's nothing revolutionary. If you're familiar with Apache Ant, this is pretty trivial. But now comes *the* question: how are these tasks defined? That's the crux of the problem and where a build system can either shine or quickly become cumbersome.

My experience is that nothing is better than scripting. Conditions, loops, and variables are absolutely necessary for any nontrivial task. So something like the following becomes possible:

```
WEB_PROJECTS = ['pie', 'soup']
foreach directory in subdirectories
   if directory in WEB_PROJECTS
      war directory
   else
      jar directory
   end
end
```

We've found the first characteristic of our ideal build system. It must support scripting and should allow us to use simple commands fitting our needs when dealing with Java.

We can even push this a little further by using a well-known concept: a *domain-specific language* (DSL for lazy writers like me). Saying the same thing differently, it's a language that must have been tailored to express the main concepts of a domain using its own terminology. The DSL approach is more and more seductive to many people, as it usually leads to a terse, natural, and very efficient language.

Using a DSL approach, the previous scripting example could be rewritten like this:

```
module 'pie' {
   type war
}
module 'soup' {
   type war
}
module 'cake' {
   type jar
}
```

What we want is a Java build DSL, but it's also more than that. For example, Ant is a DSL, even if the syntax isn't quite there. The problem is its lack of extensibility outside the main grammar defined by Ant. Ideally, you should be able to use a more powerful (even if lower level) language when the original DSL doesn't quite cut it. This is the main propriety

of an *internal* DSL, which is defined inside a more generic language (see Martin Fowler's "Domain Specific Language" at http://www.martinfowler.com/bliki/DomainSpecificLanguage.html).
Now our need is fully identified: a Java build internal DSL.

No App Is an Island: Dependencies

So what do we want of our DSL? Well, we've covered that pretty well already. It should handle basic Java tasks natively, using simple commands, and should allow us to write more complex tasks using scripting. What a beautiful tool!

Unfortunately, the world isn't that simple. Just when we're ready to claim victory, life brings us new challenges. And in the Java world, this challenge has a name: the *classpath*.

Would you want to develop your own logging framework? You own XML parser? Your own web server? What a mean job to do when you know this has already been done beautifully by other talented people. Let's open the door to all these brilliant pieces of software and welcome them as part of our own program!

But inviting many guests has a price, and in the development world, the currency is called maintenance. Software with many dependencies is hard to maintain. First, you need to install the dependencies. But how do you get all these guys? Do you have to go all over the place to retrieve them one by one? And then, even after you've found them, they still have their own life. New versions are produced. Upgrades are needed. And they have the bad habit of bringing new dependencies, as they're also reusing other brilliant pieces of software. All these pieces quickly start reusing each other, leading to diamond dependency situations (that is, A depends on B and C; B and C both depend on D) that become hard to solve, especially when you throw in different versions. It's quite a mess, really. Our ideal system needs to clean that up.

Note ➡ When I explain the way external project dependencies are used (in the following chapters), I'll always use the word *dependency*. I'll also talk about task dependencies when writing your build scripts, which are completely different. To refer to this second type of dependency, I'll use the word *prerequisite*.

Luckily, we already have a weapon: our brand-new DSL. So we probably would add a couple of words to declare external project dependencies, because we need to make things explicit (even in a dream world, computers can't guess your thoughts reliably).

```
add dependencies 'cracker', 'butter', 'egg', 'creme fraiche'
add more dependencies 'cream cheese', 'lemon'
```

How does this help? First, the build system should be able to get these dependencies "automagically." It's a lot of responsibility, but it can be done. Second, the build system should help us in dealing with versions. So, by default, it should get the latest versions of everything. And when we want to use a specific version, we should have a way to specify it:

```
add dependency 'bordeaux' (1998)
```

I can see some of my readers frowning deeply now. I can hear you say, "What? Install all these things all over on my computer? We're trading one mess for another!" Don't worry—this ideal system uses a local repository, which is a unique place where all installed software is arranged neatly. And it provides tools to easily install, reinstall, update, or delete any dependency, because we must stay in control! We can't give all the responsibilities to a computer, even if it's running an ideal build system!

More on Dreams

I don't know about you, but I loved this chapter. Dreaming is one of my favorite parts in software development, even if it's probably not a good idea to tell that to a manager. It's one of those exciting moments where ideas flow and things start shaping up as you would like them to be. Of course, you know that disappointment will come later. You'll have to face hard trade-offs and cope with inevitable limitations of your environment. But remembering the dream always brings you to things as they should be and lets you see the bigger picture.

So the build dreams brought in very interesting ideas. First, we want a Java DSL that will bring us both expressiveness and focus. Second, we need an efficient way to cope with dependencies. As you will see in the rest of this book, for a build system to be totally usable, we will need much more than that. But these two are the building blocks that provide the robustness of the whole structure.

Raven Takes Off

Let thy speech be short, understanding much in a few words . . .

Apocrypha

Now that I've explained my dream, it's time to get back to reality. But I have done my best to make the reality of Raven as close as possible to that dream. I'll sum up how in this chapter and will go into greater detail throughout the rest of this book.

The build system DSL is implemented with Rake. Rake gives you simple ways to define tasks and lets you write small scripts in Ruby. Of course, Rake is written in Ruby. So why do we need Raven if Rake does it all? Rake is generic; it has many tricks to make a build easy but nothing specific to Java. So Raven adds more words to the Rake vocabulary to make the life of Java programmers easier. In this chapter, you'll see how this works as we go through some practical examples

The Mandatory Installation Guide

Before we start doing anything, it would be pretty useful if you had Raven working on your computer. Raven doesn't have that many dependencies: Ruby, RubyGems, and Rake. That's pretty much all you're going to need.

There are currently two main Ruby interpreters: the original one created and still developed by Yukihiro (Matz) Matsumoto (written in C) and JRuby.

JRuby allows you to call Java directly within your Ruby scripts, with very good interoperability. So if you plan to extend the build with some Java code or use existing Java build extensions, you will need JRuby. It's also useful if you want to distribute your software (with its build) to many other developers. JRuby doesn't require you to install anything—it's just a zip file to unpack. So any Java developers (assuming that they have a Java Virtual Machine installed) can run it easily.

The original interpreter, CRuby, is much faster than JRuby (although JRuby is catching up, at the time I'm writing this, it's not there yet). The difference is most evident at startup—JRuby takes a long time to load. So if you don't care about Java operability at the build level, you will want to use CRuby, since Raven will run much faster under it.

The Native Ruby Way

The first item to install is the Ruby interpreter. The easiest way is to use a binary package already compiled for your platform:

- **Windows users:** Download the Ruby one-click installer (http://rubyforge.org/projects/rubyinstaller/). It not only contains Ruby, but also includes RubyGems, Rake, and many other goodies that I'm sure you will find useful. So you can even skip the coming installation steps until we get to Raven.

- **Linux users:** Most distributions' packaging systems already make Ruby available. Fedora users should issue the following command:

  yum install ruby

  Debian and Ubuntu users should use this command:

  apt-get install ruby

  If your distribution doesn't include any easy-to-use package installation system, just use rpmfind (http://www.rpmfind.net) to download the RPM and install it.

- **Mac users:** Ruby 1.8.2 comes preinstalled with version 10.4.8 (Tiger).

Once you have Ruby, you will need RubyGems. RubyGems is really a must-have when using Ruby, as it makes the installation of any tool so much easier. Download RubyGems (http://rubyforge.org/projects/rubygems/) and unpack the distribution in any directory. Open a command into that directory and type this:

ruby setup.rb

Simple, isn't it? And yes, the RubyGems installer is written in Ruby.

We've finished the hardest part. Now that RubyGems is installed, every subsequent installation becomes a single command (note that under Linux, these usually require root privileges).

Installing Rake is as simple as this:

gem install rake

And finally, install Raven like this:

gem install raven

You're all set!

The JRuby Way

JRuby is an open source project (just like the native Ruby interpreter) that implements a pure Java implementation of a Ruby interpreter. It has been trying to catch up to the native interpreter, and it's now getting fairly mature and gaining more momentum, principally in the Java community. Besides being a Ruby interpreter, JRuby is a very interesting project because it bridges Ruby and Java. Using JRuby, it's possible to access your Java classes and objects within Ruby code.

The great advantage is that you don't need to install any native code to run JRuby, as you probably already have a Java Virtual Machine (JVM) installed on your machine. To run JRuby, you just need to download the distribution and unpack it somewhere on your hard drive.

To make things even easier, Raven has a packaged JRuby installation in addition to the gem. It's the standard JRuby distribution, but RubyGems, Rake, and Raven are already bundled in it.

To install the Raven JRuby distribution, follow these steps:

1. Download the latest JRuby Raven distribution (it should be named raven-1.x.x-jruby-0.9.x.zip) from the Raven RubyForge page at http://rubyforge.org/projects/raven/.

2. Unzip the file somewhere on your file system.

3. Set the JRUBY_HOME environment variable to the directory where you've extracted the distribution.

4. Add JRUBY_HOME/bin to your PATH.

Just as a sanity check, you can run the following command, which will simply display the current time:

```
jruby -e "puts Time.now"
```

That's it! You can now run the JRuby interpreter, Rake, RubyGems, and Raven directly from the command line. All the scripts are contained in the bin directory of the distribution. The most basic is the jruby batch file, which will start the JRuby interpreter and execute the provided script.

Your First Rakefile

As I mentioned at the beginning of this chapter, Rake is a DSL specialized for building software. It introduces the notion of tasks in Ruby scripts and structures the way you write your build scripts. That's a nice theory, but let's see it in action.

I know writers who have been banned from the publishing industry because they did not include a Hello World example in their book. So, obviously, I must comply and provide the required Hello World code sample.

You tell Rake which tasks you would like to execute through a small script file called a *rakefile*. Begin by creating an empty directory somewhere on your file system and placing a file named rakefile in that directory (it could also be named Rakefile, rakefile.rb, or Rakefile.rb). Paste the following text in this rakefile:

```
require 'rake'

desc 'Says hello'
task 'hello' do
    puts 'Hello World'
end
```

Now open a command console in the directory you've just created and type this:

```
%> rake hello
```

Hello World

And the magic happens. So let's see what we just did.

The first line in the rakefile is a standard Ruby command asking the Ruby interpreter to load a library. Here, we're loading Rake. This shouldn't cause any problems, as we already installed the Rake gem.

Then we go on to the declaration of a new task and we call it 'hello'. A *task* here is simply a named piece of code that can be executed.

Everything between the do and the end is the body of our task, and we could place any Ruby code there. What we put in the body is the puts command, which is basically the same as a print command. It just adds a carriage return at the end of the line.

Finally, the rake command you entered at the command line calls our rakefile and executes the task hello.

Tip ➡ Ruby also allows you to define a block of code inside curly braces, instead of the do...end syntax. So if you like being terse and enjoy symbols more than words, you'll prefer the following: task 'hello' { puts 'Hello World' }.

There's one more item in our little example that I didn't mention yet: the desc command. What does it do? It just provides a description for the task that follows. And what is it for? Another easy question, and you can check that out yourself. Just type this:

```
%> rake --tasks
```

```
rake hello  # Says hello
```

In addition to witnessing the usefulness of the desc command, you've just learned about one of the numerous Rake options. The --tasks option lists all the documented tasks of a rakefile. It's quite handy when you have forgotten what a task does or just downloaded a project and don't know how to use it. Rake supports many different options. To learn more about them, use the --help option. It will bring you some nice reading.

For those of you who didn't quite see what I meant when I was talking about a DSL, this should start making sense now. You've just learned two very important words in the Rake vocabulary:

- task creates a callable task that you can invoke from the command line.
- desc creates a description for these tasks.

You will learn many other words in this book—some from the Rake vocabulary and many from the Raven one (still to be discovered).

Building Something Real

Our journey within Raven officially begins. You're going to see your first officially approved Raven task very soon. And to demonstrate the usage of Raven, we'll use some real-world Java code. (I don't have the heart to force you to type a full Java project just to demonstrate compilation.) We're going to create a full build script for the Commons Collections project, which is a widely used collection framework that extends the classic Java collection framework. This project is open source and developed within the Apache Software Foundation. But what it really does isn't relevant for our purpose. It's just a Java project with a small but still significant codebase. And it's simple enough to use as a first build example.

Compiling

To download the sources of Commons Collections, go to the project web page (http://jakarta.apache.org/commons/collections/), click the download link in the menu bar, and select the latest source distribution. (I've used Commons Collections version 3.2 to write this example, so you might want to stick with that version just in case later versions include some incompatible changes.) You should obtain a file named commons-collections-x.x-src.zip. Unzip this file in the directory of your choice.

We'll start with the first thing everyone does: compiling. Create a file named rakefile in the root directory for Commons Collections with the following content:

```
require 'raven'

javac 'compile' do |task|
   task.build_path << "src/java"
end
```

Then open a command console in the same directory and type this:

```
%> rake compile
```

This should compile all the project sources and place them in a target/classes directory. Go ahead and check it out. You'll see that I'm not lying.

As you can see, our script first requires Raven, which loads Raven extensions in the Ruby interpreter. And then we use our first Raven task: javac. The javac task is an extension to the classic Rake task that runs the javac program to compile Java source files. We're therefore creating a javac task named compile (which we call later using rake).

But there's probably something that looks slightly strange to your Java programmer's eyes (unless you're already a Ruby programmer): |task|. What does that mean? It's a Ruby notation that creates a temporary variable available in the body of the task. In this case, the variable here will hold a reference to the task itself. It's very useful because it lets you configure the task before it executes by setting attributes of the task directly.

In this example, we're setting the build_path attribute, which is the path the javac task will build. The default value for this path is src/main/java. So if you place your sources in this subdirectory of your project directory, you won't need any customization and will be able to use the javac task in its simplest form:

```
javac 'compile'
```

The Commons Collections project chose to place its sources in the src/java directory, making this bit of configuration necessary.

Note ➡ Raven has been built from the ground up to be as terse as possible. It uses many default values without limiting the possibilities or making your life harder. Most (if not all) of these default values can be customized and overridden. This keeps things simple but also makes more exotic usages as easy as possible. I don't believe that there's only one way to organize your project or even that there's a single best way. Raven's flexibility reflects this belief.

The build_path attribute can actually contain more than one path, as it's an array. Maybe you've been wondering why we've set the build path using << instead of simply using the = operator. The << operator means "add into." It's the same functionality as calling the add() method on a Java collection. So it's possible to add several directories in the build_path attribute if your project is structured with several submodules in the source directory. For example, you could have this:

```
javac 'compile' do |t|
    t.build_path << "src/java/dao"
    t.build_path << "src/java/service"
    t.build_path << "src/java/web"
end
```

But wait! Our tasks should be plain Ruby, right? So instead of writing so much code, why don't we try to find something shorter and more flexible using neat scripting? In that case, the previous code excerpt could be replaced by this:

```
javac 'compile' do |t|
    t.build_path << Dir.glob('src/java/*')
end
```

That's so much better! And that's your first real scripting usage in a rakefile. I'll provide more examples throughout this book. And don't forget that when you find something painful to write, chances are that there's a smarter and enjoyable way using Ruby.

I still owe you an explanation of what the standard Ruby function Dir.glob exactly does. For those of you familiar with Ant, it's a bit like building a fileset. It just returns an array of directory or file paths selected using the pattern you're passing. This pattern can be composed of regular directory names, but it also may contain most of the wildcards you can think of, such as *, **, and ?.

Tip ➡ Ruby, being a very flexible language as well, lets you opt for the even shorter notation and use a neat one-liner (here the parentheses around the task name are necessary, you will understand why later): javac('compile') { |t| t.build_path << Dir.glob('src/java/*') }.

Putting It in a JAR

Usually, after compiling a module, you'll be interested in bundling the compiled classes in a JAR file. This may be because you want to distribute it, copy it somewhere else and include it in a classpath, or for another reason. Producing this JAR file is also a single task. Just include the following declaration at the end of the rakefile we've created for Commons Collections:

```
jar 'collections.jar' => 'compile'
```

Then execute the following command:

```
rake collections.jar
```

Just check the result in the target subdirectory created by Raven. In that directory, you will find a file named collections.jar, just like the task name. Raven is simply taking all the compiled classes and packaging them in the JAR.

The jar task can also be configured to use a manifest file. Here is an example:

```
jar 'collections.jar' => 'compile' do |t|
    t.manifest = 'src/resources/manifest.mf'
end
```

There's a piece of notation here that you haven't seen before. After the task name is this strange addition: => 'compile'. This expresses task prerequisites. As I mentioned earlier, Rake is a pretty sophisticated build tool. It provides the infrastructure most builds will need. So you can declare that a task depends on another task or set of tasks. Rake will make sure to execute those other tasks and to execute them only once per build to avoid redundancy. To declare more than one prerequisite for a task, use an array instead or a simple string, like this:

```
jar 'collections.jar' => ['prepare', 'compile']
```

Note ➡ You've probably observed during your Java developments that compiling and creating JARs can be time consuming, especially on large source trees. If you have many files to compile and put in a JAR, it can get very CPU- and I/O-intensive. So most Raven tasks, like javac and jar, check for modifications before being executed. The javac task will start the javac command only if there are modified files, and jar will start only if the JAR isn't up-to-date. This is a feature of all build tools, not just Raven.

Finally, it's usually a good idea to have a default task in your rakefile. This way, if someone just executes Rake without passing a task, a sensible default will be executed automatically. To make the jar task your default, just add the following in your rakefile:

```
task 'default' => 'collections.jar'
```

The default task is the one automatically executed by Rake when no task is provided. With this line, you add the collections.jar tasks as a prerequisite, so Rake will execute it first.

What's Up, Doc (Ruby Doc, That Is)?

As you're a zealous developer, you've probably been careful to include nice Javadoc comments in your code. And you will surely want to make the Javadoc generation part of your build. That's easy!

```
javadoc('jdoc') { |t| t.build_path = 'src/java' }
```

Just as for the javac task, we've set the build_path attribute to match the one used by Commons Collections. But again, if your sources are in src/main/java, that's not needed. I think by now you know which command you need to type to execute the task, so I'll let you test it. The generated Javadoc can be found in the target/jdoc directory.

Going to War Peacefully: WAR Files

The last Raven task I'm going to tell you about in this chapter is the war task. As you might have guessed already, its goal is to build a web archive (WAR) file. Why create a task only for that? After all, a WAR is just a JAR with an extension starting with w? The answer is that a WAR is supposed to have a certain internal layout, and Raven helps you build that layout easily.

Unfortunately, I won't be able to demonstrate this with Commons Collections as in the previous examples, as this project is a library. But here is the simplest example:

```
war 'doodle.war' => 'compile'
```

This assumes that you've followed Raven's defaults of placing all your web resources in the src/main/webapp subdirectory. This command takes these web resources (so you will probably want to have your web.xml under src/main/webapp/WEB-INF) and includes them in the created WAR. It will also take the compiled classes of this module and place them in the WAR under WEB-INF/classes. Finally, it will take all your project external dependencies to put them in WEB-INF/lib. I can already hear you saying, "Dependencies? Which dependencies?" Just a little patience my dear reader; there will be much more on that in the next chapter.

As with all Raven tasks, war can be configured to use any web resources directory of your choice. So if you don't want to play by the defaults, you can do this:

```
war('doodle.war') => 'compile' { |t| webapp_dir='src/webapp' }
```

We've been running through this chapter at a pretty high pace. Let's pause and think a bit about a couple of missing pieces. There are things that I didn't tell you yet about all these tasks (I can be sneaky sometimes), and now is the right time for an examination of what's under the hood.

The True Nature of Tasks

I've shown you how to configure Raven tasks by setting one of their properties in what I've called the *body* of your task, or a block. And I have mentioned briefly that these blocks can contain any Ruby code. But let's see what's behind. A *block* is actually a very powerful concept available in Ruby to provide pieces of code.

A block can be described as an anonymous piece of code. It's just delimited by do...end or {..}. It wouldn't be really useful as such if it couldn't be passed around, but fortunately, it can.

Thanks to blocks, Ruby can implement very powerful and short iteration idioms but also much more:

```
3.times { puts "I love chocolate!"}
developers.select {|developer| developer.skills.size > 2 }
Dir.chdir('far/reaching/dir') do
    # This executes in the subdirectory but the
    # initial directory will be restored afterward
end
```

Tip ➡ Blocks can even become closures and be stored in variables to be reused later. The "Containers, Blocks and Iterators" chapter of *The Pragmatic Programmers Guide* (http://www.rubycentral.com/book/tut_containers.html) provides some interesting read on that subject.

A typical example of customizing tasks by adding some standard Ruby code in them could be to include additional resources in a JAR. Many projects have that type of need, as it allows you to load files (property files, XML files, and so on) easily from the classpath. Here is how this could be achieved with the jar task:

```
jar 'collections.jar' => 'compile' do
    FileUtils.cp(Dir.glob('resources/*.*'), 'target/classes')
end
```

This should give you an idea of how the power of Ruby scripting can help you in building your tasks easily and quickly. Any Ruby code can be inserted in a task body and will be executed before the task really starts doing its job (here, before the JAR file is built). The jar task body in this example includes FileUtils and Dir.glob. Dir.glob(. . .), which you have seen already, will list all the files in the resources directory. FileUtils includes many utility methods to manipulate files: copying, deleting, moving, and so on. (The RDoc for FileUtils can be found at http://www.ruby-doc.org/stdlib/libdoc/fileutils/rdoc/index.html.)

But that's not all. There's definitely more to a task than what it seems at first. There's a grand treachery going on undercover—something that has been right under your eyes but that almost no one could have guessed. Let me unveil this secret for you: a task definition is a method call. That's right—a simple method call. No magic, nothing unnatural, and no groundbreaking constructs are involved. It's just a classic method call.

Using the preceding example to illustrate, consider the jar task declaration that also copies resources. The name of the method is jar, of course, but what are the parameters? That's a Ruby trick. The parentheses in parameter passing aren't mandatory; they can be omitted in most cases. Another trick is the usage of the => operator. It can be used to create a hash (in Java terminology, a *map*) on the fly. The 'collections.jar' => 'compile' part of the declaration effectively creates a hash with a single key/value pair. The key is the task name, and the value is its dependencies. So the preceding example is strictly equivalent to this:

```
jar(Hash['collections.jar', 'compile']) do
    FileUtils.cp_r(Dir.glob('resources/*.*'), 'target/classes')
end
```

There's still one mystery left in this declaration. What about the block provided after the method call? That certainly doesn't look like a standard method call. Let's see how the jar method signature looks in Raven. That should help you to guess what's happening.

def jar(args, &block)

Yes, you guessed right. The block is passed to the method as an additional parameter. Ruby has a class to represent blocks (named Proc), and that representation is passed to the method. The & notation just tells Ruby that you're expecting a block.

So, in short, what's happening behind the scenes is the following:

- Rake loads and executes your whole script in the same way that any Ruby script would be loaded—nothing fancy about the execution itself.

- The tasks declared in your script are actually method calls resulting in the creation of task objects in memory. The provided block is associated with the task.

- Rake analyzes the prerequisites of the task you called from the command line, executes these tasks (which, in turn, execute the block that has been associated with them, if there is one), and finally executes the task you've called (also executing its block).

That's a rough sketch to give you the idea. Now you won't be fooled anymore because you know what's really happening. There's no magic—just simple method calls and the beauty of Ruby.

RAVEN ISN'T RUBY MAVEN

I've talked about all the default values that Raven uses for its tasks. I must confess that I didn't invent these defaults. They come from another Java build project named Maven. Those of you who are familiar with this project probably noticed it already.

I've used the same defaults as Maven for two principal reasons:

- Maven is a popular build project for Java developers. I wanted to ease the transition of existing projects to Raven.

- These defaults exist and make sense. There might be better ones, but there are also many worse ones. I don't believe in a single best solution that applies to all projects. So these defaults are good enough for most projects. If they don't work for you, they're easy to change.

You will see other similarities between Maven and Raven in the following chapters, especially for dependency management. But don't be mistaken. These similarities are only present where I thought they made sense. Raven is a build tool for Java based on Ruby, and more specifically, Rake and RubyGems. These are its foundations. Raven is absolutely not a Ruby version of Maven. It solves the same problems, but does so very differently.

Summary

Table 2-1 lists the tasks I've introduced in this chapter, plus an additional one (jar_source) that doesn't require much explanation provided all the knowledge you've already gained.

Table 2-1. Java Tasks Reference

Task	Properties (Default)	Description
javac	build_path (src/main/java)	Compiles your Java sources and places the compiled classes in the target/classes directory
jar	manifest (none)	Packages your compiled classes in a JAR archive with the same name as your task
jar_source	build_path (src/main/java)	Packages your sources in a JAR archive with the same name as your task
javadoc	build_path (src/main/java)	Generates the Javadoc for your project in the target/jdoc directory
war	webapp_dir (src/main/webapp)	Creates a WAR archive for your project including the web resources, classes, and libraries

There's really a lot of information in this chapter. After dreaming of the skeleton of a build system, we've started putting some meat on those bones, and Raven is taking shape.

You've seen your first rakefile, and I've shown you how these files are structured and what they do. I've explained the core Java tasks that Raven provides—what they do and how to configure them. Finally, there have been some revelations about the way Rake works and what the tasks really are. We're just using simple method calls.

All of these put us in an ideal situation to start injecting some blood in this body. Eventually, you will see Raven come to life and move.

CHAPTER 3

Wait, I Have Dependencies!

I do not know what I may appear to the world; but to myself I seem to have been only like a boy playing on the seashore, and diverting myself in now and then finding a smoother pebble or a prettier shell than ordinary, whilst the great ocean of truth lay all undiscovered before me.

Isaac Newton

So far, we've been working in an ideal world. The birds were singing, the sun was shining, and all was perfect. I've even heard that while you were reading the previous chapters, all the wars in the world stopped. Sadly, I must remind you of the cruel brutality of the real world. I wouldn't want to leave you unprepared at the end of this book.

In reality, you will very rarely deal with an isolated project that doesn't use any external libraries. And despite what I just said about brutality, using existing code is actually a pretty good thing. We don't have any time to lose in redoing what has already been done before. We must move on! So your project has dependencies, and usually that also means more problems.

Dependency management in Raven relies on RubyGems, which is a package management system. It wraps programs and libraries in small bundles called gems, and offers a lot of services to install and manage these gems. RubyGems is a really powerful and efficient system. Raven reuses it and wraps Java JARs into a gem. All your programs, as well as the ones they depend on, become gems. And that solves a lot of problems fairly elegantly. But as always, Raven gives you choices. If you prefer, you can handle all your libraries yourself, rather than use a dependency management system.

In this chapter, we'll take a closer look at RubyGems, and then focus on how to use it to handle dependencies with Raven.

The Jewelry Business: RubyGems

The Ruby world is full of precious discoveries, and the first one of them is unquestionably RubyGems. Don't worry—I'm not going to lecture you on the different types of minerals and their chemical structures. As I just said, RubyGems is a package management system. You may have heard of the Linux package managers called rpms and debs and some of their respective management tools, like yum and apt-get. If that previous sentence sounds like gibberish to you, then you'll find the following explanations helpful.

Brilliance: How RubyGems Works

A package management system (let's call it a PMS from now on, not to be mistaken for a dangerous feminine syndrome) is a tool that helps you install, update, search, get information about, update, and uninstall packages. But you might be wondering exactly what a *package* is. A package is a file that contains everything necessary to install a given program or library. The most simple example of a package is a zip file containing a given program. But usually packages contain at least a descriptor file that the PMS can use to get more information about them.

RubyGems is a PMS, and a package is called a *gem*. With RubyGems, to install a software package, you can simply do this (as you saw in the Raven installation chapter):

```
gem install raven
```

This instruction triggers several actions:

- **Look up the package in the gem index:** RubyGems synchronizes its *gem index* and looks up the Raven gems in it. To be able to search among all the gems offered by a repository as large as RubyForge (4,429 at the time of writing), RubyGems uses an index file. This file is automatically downloaded the first time you run RubyGems, and then synchronized on subsequent usages if it has changed. Then the search is performed on your local copy.

- **Download from the gem repository:** When the gem has been found, it downloads the gem file from the central *gem repository*. To download and install all the gems you need, RubyGems uses a central repository hosting all these files. The default repository used by a standard installation of RubyGems is hosted by RubyForge (http://www.rubyforge.org). Most of the gems you will ever need are available there.

Note ➡ You can create your own gem repository if you want to distribute your own gems. I'll show you how to do this in Chapter 5.

- **Install the gem:** RubyGems installs the gem in your local Ruby directory tree under a gem directory that will be your local gem repository,

RubyGems handles dependencies for you. So, if you're installing something that requires other libraries, it tries to install them as well. But it will ask your permission first; RubyGems always stays polite and well-mannered.

RubyGems also can manage more than one version of the same gem. This means that having different programs or libraries using different versions of the same package isn't really a problem—until they're both used at the same time; in which case, RubyGems will complain.

~~JAVA~~ RDOC

RDoc is the Ruby equivalent of Javadoc. It's just four letters, as Ruby people like short names. It generates a full web site that can be browsed easily to get the code documentation. And as Ruby is open source at its core, some RDoc sites even publish the code in-line inside the documentation (the Rails RDoc, for example)!

The most helpful RDoc site is probably the one for Ruby itself: http://ruby-doc.org/core/. You can generate the RDoc for any Ruby program that you've downloaded just by executing the rdoc command from its root directory.

If you're tempted to try some (or more) Ruby programming, you can learn more about RDoc (and how to format comments in your code to have them nicely published) at http://rdoc.sourceforge.net/.

As for Raven, all the RDoc documentation is available at http://raven.rubyforge.org/doc/.

Crafting: Using RubyGems

You got your first experience with RubyGems in the previous chapter, when you installed Raven and Rake. Now let's try some practical exploration.

I always try out the help of a new command-line tool to start. A nice help often means a painless experience. Also, it's a really quick way to get an overview of what the command can do. So let's try it out:

```
%> gem --help
```

```
RubyGems is a sophisticated package manager for Ruby.  This is a
basic help message containing pointers to more information.

  Usage:
    gem -h/--help
    gem -v/--version
    gem command [arguments...] [options...]
```

Examples:
  gem install rake
  gem list --local
  gem build package.gemspec
  gem help install

Further help:
  gem help commands   list all 'gem' commands
  gem help examples   show some examples of usage
  gem help <COMMAND>   show help on COMMAND
                    (e.g. 'gem help install')
Further information:
  http://rubygems.rubyforge.org

The examples give a good sense of the most simple tasks: install a gem, get a list of all gems, build your own gem, and get help. But the "Further help" section hints at much more. I won't go into the details of each gem command, but asking for the list of commands with their description provides a pretty good overview:

%> gem help commands

GEM commands are:

build	Build a gem from a gemspec
cert	Adjust RubyGems certificate settings
check	Check installed gems
cleanup	Cleanup old versions of installed gems in the local repository
contents	Display the contents of the installed gems
dependency	Show the dependencies of an installed gem
environment	Display RubyGems environmental information
help	Provide help on the 'gem' command
install	Install a gem into the local repository
list	Display all gems whose name starts with STRING
query	Query gem information in local or remote repositories
rdoc	Generates RDoc for pre-installed gems
search	Display all gems whose name contains STRING
specification	Display gem specification (in yaml)
uninstall	Uninstall a gem from the local repository
unpack	Unpack an installed gem to the current directory
update	Update the named gem (or all installed gems) in the local repository

For help on a particular command, use 'gem help COMMAND'.

Commands may be abbreviated, so long as they are unambiguous.
e.g. 'gem i rake' is short for 'gem install rake'.

As you can see, the command-line help is straightforward. The only notion requiring some explanation is the *gemspec*. The gemspec is the descriptor file that is bundled with every single gem. It specifies all the required information about the gem, including its name, version, author name, the dependencies, a description, the eventual inclusion of an executable file, and other elements. You can take a look at the Raven gemspec by typing this:

%> gem specification raven

A command I find interesting is environment. It just tells you where RubyGems is installed on your system, the current version, the current central repository, and where all the gems are installed. Here is how it looks on my system:

%> gem environment

```
Rubygems Environment:
  - VERSION: 0.9.0 (0.9.0)
  - INSTALLATION DIRECTORY: /usr/lib/ruby/gems/1.8
  - GEM PATH:
    - /usr/lib/ruby/gems/1.8
  - REMOTE SOURCES:
    - http://gems.rubyforge.org
```

From here, I think you can find your way around. Feel free to experiment. Everything that you install can be uninstalled, And everything that you uninstall can be reinstalled. So you're pretty much covered.

Raven Gets Brilliant: Handling Dependencies

Yes, I know, all these puns with RubyGems are getting annoying. But you should feel lucky when compared to the poor readers of REST web services books. Besides, I really can't help it.

You've probably guessed by now that all this talk about RubyGems wasn't just for fun and that Raven makes some use of it. You've guessed right. With such a nice packaging system, why reinvent the wheel? As I'm a pretty lazy guy, I just wrapped Raven around RubyGems to reuse all the goodies.

Here, I'll detail what you can do using Raven commands and dependency declarations. But keep in mind that under the hood, there's a gem, so you can always make use of RubyGems.

Note ➡ The coming paragraphs are all about installing gems explicitly. There's also a way with Raven to install dependencies automatically—download and installation will happen when Raven decides it needs something. However, I've always believed that before using some magic, it's better to know what's really going on. Magicians don't want you to learn their tricks so they abuse your eyes, but the objective of this book is precisely to let you learn them all. So for now, we're going to stick with explicit installations. I'll cover automation in Chapter 5.

Installing Dependencies

Let's start with an example:

```
%> raven install log4j
```

This will effectively install the latest version of log4j as a gem on your machine in the gems installation directory. However, this should be the origin of an endless puzzlement on your side. Installing a gem? But log4j is a Java JAR! And where did Raven get log4j in the first place? And how did it find it? So many questions and so little time.

Raven finds all Java libraries in Maven repositories, which publish most of the JARs produced by open source Java projects. But if you're a bit familiar with Maven, you'll know that it's a little more complex than it seems. Maven repositories are structured with group IDs, artifact IDs, and version numbers that can make finding something a tad complex. So Raven needs a way to search these.

To provide this functionality, I've built indexes for Maven repositories. These just list all libraries published in a Maven repository with the required information, and they are synchronized once a week with the original. You can see them on Raven's site at http://raven.rubyforge.org/indices/. This way, Raven can try to be smart about your request and save you some brainpower for other problems more interesting to solve.

So when you execute raven install, Raven first synchronizes its local indexes with the ones published on Raven's site. It just downloads them if they don't exist yet or if they're outdated. Then it performs the search and downloads what it has found from the corresponding repository.

But how smart can Raven be? Let's find out by trying to confuse it a bit:

```
%> raven install commons-db
```

Couldn't install a gem from name commons-db, more than one potential
gem was found for this name. If this is intentional and you want to
install all these gems please run again with the --all option.
    commons-dbutils v1.0 (project commons-dbutils)
    commons-dbcp v1.2.1-nojdbc3 (project commons-dbcp)

Even when you're trying to abuse it, Raven stays polite.

When Raven finds an exact match for the string you've entered, it proceeds with installation. If it can't find anything, it will try to search libraries that include the provided string in their name. If only one is found, all is nice and dandy, and Raven can install it. If more than one library is found, Raven tells you about the problem. Then you basically have two choices: you can provide a more specific query or you can install all the found libraries. In the latter case, using the --all option will do the trick.

I've answered some of the initial questions that you might have, but the main mystery remains. How can a JAR become a gem? It's fine to download a JAR from a Maven repository, but a JAR will remain a JAR. No, I didn't hide a computerized version of Houdini in the Raven code. What happens is that Raven wraps the JAR file into a gem on the fly. It's just constructing a gemspec (descriptor file) and packaging the JAR properly with it to obtain a gem. And then Raven asks RubyGems to install this gem, as it would with any other gem.

However, sometimes just a library name or something that sounds like a library name isn't enough to fulfill all of your installation needs. For those other needs, more options are available.

SERVE YOUR GEMS

Installing gems is fine, but it can lead to fairly big local repositories, especially with Raven, as each JAR becomes a gem (and Java loves to multiply the JAR count). RubyGems provides many tools to help you list and manage the gems, but you'll often wish for an easy way to have them listed outside a console. No need to wish! It already exists. Just run this:

gem_server

Then open a browser at http://localhost:8808/ and see the magic happen!

Choosing a Version

The most basic need besides the installation of the gem itself is to choose a specific version. Raven always tries to guess the latest version number when none is provided, which often makes life easier. I said "tries," because Maven is pretty lax about the versions that can be published in its repositories, and ordering them can sometimes become hard.

If you want a specific version, provide it after the gem name, preceded by a colon:

%> raven install log4j:1.2.6

To see all the versions available for a given library, enter this:

%> raven --allversions log4j

Couldn't install a gem from name log4j, more than one potential
gem was found for this name. If this is intentional and you want to
install all these gems please run again with the --all option.
   log4j v1.1.3 (project log4j)
   log4j v1.2.4 (project log4j)
   log4j v1.2.5 (project log4j)
   log4j v1.2.6 (project log4j)
   log4j v1.2.7 (project log4j)
   log4j v1.2.8 (project log4j)
   log4j v1.2.9 (project log4j)
   log4j v1.2.11 (project log4j)
   log4j v1.2.12 (project log4j)
   log4j v1.2.13 (project log4j)

This option can also be shortened to -v.

Installing a Project

Some projects like to split their sources across several modules. It's pretty nice for development, but for project users, it's a bit of a pain, as you need to rely on several JARs instead of just one. The --project option comes to the rescue to let you install everything that a project published. However, this option will select more than one gem, so you need to add --all or -a to let Raven know that you know about the multiple gems.

%> raven install --project axis2 -a

The --project option can also be used when you want to be explicit about the project to which a given JAR belongs. Some projects aren't too original and use identical JAR names, and these cases require disambiguation. Here's an example:

```
%> raven install commons-logging
```

Couldn't install a gem from name commons-logging, more than one potential
gem was found for this name. If this is intentional and you want to
install all these gems please run again with the --all option.
    commons-logging v4.0.6 (project tomcat)
    commons-logging v1.1 (project commons-logging)

In that specific case, the --project option is necessary to pick the right library.

Note ➡ If you're running Raven behind a corporate proxy, that shouldn't be a problem. The --proxy or -p
option comes to the rescue. Use the full proxy URL—something like
http://*username:password@proxyhost:port*.

We've been installing libraries like crazy. But strangely enough, you still don't know
how to use all these JARs, wrapped in gems as they are. You've seen how to use Raven to
write simple build scripts. You've seen how to use Raven to install dependencies. Bringing
the two together is coming up next.

Surrendering Autonomy: The dependency Task

It's time to open your builds and bring others in. Feed the monstrous and insatiable Java
classpath, even if that means surrendering your build autonomy. But don't worry—we'll
keep control, and we'll do all that with style.

So let's get back to our *rakefile*. I hope you didn't forget about it already. It's a small
script file based on named tasks that Rake executes for you. It turns out that the project
dependencies are declared there as well. And as it's still plain Ruby, so you can tweak,
manipulate, or even generate your declarations. But we'll hold off on those refinements for
the next chapter. First, let's have a peek at the dependency task:

```
dependency 'compile_deps' do |t|
    t.deps << [{'commons-logging-commons-logging' => '1.0.4'}, 'commons-pool']
    t.deps << ['commons-lang', 'wsdl4j-wsdl4j', 'log4j-log4j']
end
```

The syntax should look familiar to you by now. We're declaring a dependency task
named compile-deps. Then we configure the task by adding dependencies to it.

This example also shows two possible ways to declare a dependency: you can just provide its name and Raven will pick the latest local one, or you can provide a specific version by passing it in a hash element.

Declaring dependencies is a fine thing, but isn't that useful if you can't reference them when you compile. Luckily, using them is easy:

```
javac 'compile' => 'compile_deps'
```

Yes, it's that simple. Just add the dependency task name as a prerequisite for the task to have it use all the declared dependencies.

How does this all the work? First, when you use the javac task, Raven checks all the prerequisites. If one (or several) of them is a dependency task, Raven processes all the dependencies passed to it. That's half the way.

Now from these dependencies, it finds the gems installed in your local repository using simple name matching. Inside these gems, there's a JAR, and that JAR is appended to a classpath. Finally, the classpath is passed to the javac command executed by the task.

The last thing to note about the dependency task is that it accepts other dependency tasks as prerequisites. This is a pretty neat way to group your dependency declaration:

```
dependency 'compile_deps' => ['spring_deps', 'hibernate_deps']
```

NO SNAPSHOT POLICY

If you have some familiarity with Maven, you've probably met snapshot versions. The snapshot mechanism is a Maven feature that tries to download a dependency again anytime you build (whereas Raven always downloads only once as long as you don't explicitly upgrade versions). It's like saying, "This version is temporary. See if there's a new one anytime I build." You might have noticed that Raven always uses well-defined versions.

This snapshot feature is evil—really. And especially because it's often abused. If you rely on it, your build can get broken because it has been updated to something that doesn't work. So Raven just treats a snapshot as a normal version, except that it's version 0, so any other version will be installed preferably.

Actually javac isn't the only task that can rely on a dependency declaration. You've seen another task that could use that: the war task, introduced in the previous chapter. When I've talked about the war task, I mentioned that dependencies would be automatically packaged in the WEB-INF/lib directory of the web archive. This also works by using a dependency task as a prerequisite. In the following example, runtime_deps is a dependency task declaration:

```
war 'doodle.war' => ['compile', 'runtime_deps']
```

Building Classpaths: The lib-dir Task

So far, we've talked about building a project. Sooner or later, you will want to run it. And then you will be all by yourself, because Raven won't be there anymore. But you declared all your dependencies already! Will you have to declare them again to build your classpath at runtime? Of course not. The task that will help you is lib_dir. It's quite simple really. It just copies all your dependencies in a single directory:

```
lib_dir 'libs' => 'runtime_deps'
```

If you just declare it this way, all the libraries will be copied to a lib directory directly under your project root subdirectory. However, as with all Raven tasks, you can specify the directory into which you want the libraries to be copied:

```
lib_dir 'prepare_lib' => 'compile_deps' do |t|
    t.target = 'dist/lib'
end
```

Now you could be thinking, "It's just copying my libraries? That's a bit light. I'll still have to specify them one by one to build my runtime classpath." Actually, you won't. Most operating systems (Windows, Linux, and Unix) allow you to write simple shell scripts to add all the files in a directory to your classpath. In my experience, that's the easiest way to proceed, even if it's not really part of Raven. Complex classpath composition techniques usually end up being difficult to maintain.

For Windows, a batch file building your classpath from a library directory could look like the following (just initialize the LIB_DIR environment variable to the directory containing your libraries):

```
set CLASSPATH=%LIB_DIR%
FOR %%c in (%LIB_DIR%\*.jar) DO (call :append_cp %%c)

:append_cp
set CLASSPATH=%CLASSPATH%;%1
goto end

REM Do other things like running your program here.
:end
```

For Linux, use something like this:

```
for f in $LIB_DIR/*.jar
do
  CLASSPATH=$CLASSPATH:$f
done
```

The lib_dir task will easily prepare your directory, and by using simple scripts, you can run your program from there. You could also build a distribution using the lib_dir task; just declare it as a prerequisite of the task that will assemble the distribution.

Doing It Your Way: Adding Dependencies Explicitly

Despite all the beauty of RubyGems and the Raven installation command, you might not want to use a dependency management system. Perhaps you prefer to gather all the dependencies yourself and check them in a concurrent versioning system. Or you might need a library that isn't distributed by any repository. That shouldn't happen too often, but you will still need a way to handle those cases.

For these two reasons, Raven allows you to add JARs explicitly to a dependency declaration. It's really just like any dependency declaration, but instead of referencing gems, you are directly giving the path to a JAR or a set of JARs:

```
dependency 'spring_deps' do |t|
    t.libs << ['lib/spring-core.jar', 'lib/spring-jdbc.jar',
        'lib/spring-context.jar']
end
```

This is the totally manual method. Most of you will probably prefer the quicker method:

```
dependency 'all_deps' do |t|
    t.libs << Dir.glob('lib/**/*.*')
end
```

Alternatively, you can structure your library directory by grouping dependencies in subdirectories (for example, a subdirectory for Spring JARs, one for Hibernate JARs, and so on). This will allow you to group the JARs coming from the same source in a distinct dependency declaration using wildcards.

Test Time: The junit Task

Finally, it's time to tell you about the last Raven task that you will see in this book. That's not to say that it's going to finish soon, since I still have many things to tell you. As in all good stories, there will be love, action, drama, and a happy ending. But those will happen without a new task, as there is much more to Raven than a mere set of tasks.

After learning how to handle dependencies, you can finally run some code to test your software. This last task has, just like all others, a simple and descriptive name: junit. You've probably already guessed what it does: executes a set of JUnit test cases and tells you what breaks. If you're unfamiliar with JUnit, a really good unit test tool, check it out at http://www.junit.org. (For the moment, Raven supports only JUnit 3.*x*.)

The task declaration is pretty straightforward. Here is a classic example:

```
junit 'test' => ['compile', 'test_deps']
```

Note that the task also compiles the tests before executing them. For this reason, it inherits all the configurable properties from the javac task. The default for test selection is to pick up all the classes starting with test in the src/test/java directory. All classes selected this way will be executed as JUnit test cases.

Alternatively, you can specify which classes to test yourself:

```
junit 'test' => ['compile', 'deps', 'test_deps'] do |t|
    t.test_classes = Dir.glob("test/java/**/*Test.java")
end
```

And that's it!

Summary

In this chapter, you learned a lot about the RubyGems packaging system and how Raven relies on it to handle your project dependencies. It's just as simple as installing the needed packages (if you don't have them installed from another project already) and declaring them in your rakefile—period.

You've seen how the war task assembles the required JAR files in its WEB-INF/lib directory. You've also learned about the lib_dir task, which prepares all those libraries in a single directory to make them easy to add to your runtime classpath. With all those weapons, you're ready to conquer your Java build, and you should be able to write your first build scripts for simple or medium-complexity projects. For more information about the tasks covered so far, including the junit task that you've just seen, refer to the Raven RDoc at http://raven.rubyforge.org.

As you work with Raven, keep in mind that your build scripts should stay simple. Ruby, Rake, RubyGems, and Raven have all been built with simplicity in mind. Remember that you write your rakefiles for yourself, but chances are that sooner or later, someone else will need to read and understand them. In the following chapters, I'll show you more advanced techniques and you will see ways to cope with more complex build requirements. But don't forget the simplicity when solving them.

CHAPTER 4

Divide and Conquer: Multimodule Projects

I know not with what weapons World War III will be fought, but World War IV will be fought with sticks and stones.

Albert Einstein

We all know that tearing down boundaries and loving your fellow human beings work much better than building barriers and waging war. But when developing software, introducing some divisions and isolating parts of the code from others are usually the better approach. It shields you from spaghetti code (not that I don't like spaghetti, but only with tomato sauce or pesto).

A common practice in software engineering is to split a big project into several parts, often called *modules*. Then you can enforce which module depends on which other modules, and even more interesting, which module *can't* depend on another module. This type of modularization creates isolation between different parts of your code, making it more maintainable and avoiding the spaghetti effect. As this type of project puts more responsibilities on the build, scripts can therefore become much more complex, introducing more specificity.

To build multimodule projects, we don't need to get into fancy techniques or invent groundbreaking mechanisms. We're just going to reuse what I've shown you already: RubyGems and Rake, with just a bit of Raven in the middle for lubrication.

Modules to Gems

Let's imagine we need to develop a web site of medium size in Java. We'll call it coconut (selling coconuts on the web sounds like a damn good business). We'll split our project in three different modules: one for the persistence, one for the business logic, and one for the presentation layer (Struts actions, for example). This way, we can make sure that no one developing on our project will ever be tempted to make direct use of the persistence layer directly from the presentation. It's also a good technique to avoid circular dependencies in a project, as running separate compilations would make the compilation of a circle impossible (the first one could not be found).

We choose the following directory structure:

The presentation layer, in the web directory, depends on the business layer, which in turn depends on the persistence layer. But we don't want to introduce any direct dependency between the web module and the persistence module. Said differently, the web module shouldn't have any of the classes of the persistence module in its classpath when compiling

You already know how to build each of these modules individually, but the problem of having one module depending on the other one is still unsolved.

Once more, the solution is quite simple: we're going to build a gem from each module. Then the gem can be declared as a dependency, just as it with any other dependency. For example, the gem produced from the business module can declare as a dependency the gem produced from the persistence module

So how can you build a gem? You could use RubyGems directly. You could also use Rake; it provides a specific task to produce a gem file. But the easiest way is to use Raven, as it has been designed to handle Java-based gems. And there's a task in Raven just to build a gem for a Java project.

The name of this Raven task is gem_wrap. It wraps the JAR file(s) produced by your module in a gem that can be reused. It's really as short as this:

```
gem_wrap 'gem_persistence' => 'persistence.jar' do |t|
    t.version = '1.0'
end
```

Don't forget to declare the task that creates your JAR as a prerequisite. That's pretty important; otherwise, the produced gem could be empty. Giving the version is also very important; otherwise, the task will complain. It's one of the very few mandatory configuration settings in Raven.

This will create a gem in the target directory of your project named coconut-persistence-1.0.gem. For you, watchful reader, it should seem strange that Raven picked the name of your project and your module. These two haven't been declared anywhere, so how did Raven do that trick?

Raven just found the information where it was already: in the directory structure. The default value for the module name is the directory in which the rakefile is located. The default value for the project name is the parent directory of this directory. As most multimodule projects are structured this way, these defaults just make everyone's life easier.

But again, Raven recognizes that some people's needs may be different. You may want to structure your project directory structure in your own fashion. So explicit values can be provided, like this:

```
gem_wrap 'gem_persistence' => 'persistence.jar' do |t|
    t.project = 'coconut'
    t.artifact = 'persistence'
    t.version = '1.0'
end
```

Nice! But there are a lot of hard-coded values here. What would be the point of using a cool scripting language like Ruby if we're just hard-coding everything? Say that we want to name our project as the directory two levels up from our module directory, rather than one level up. How would that look? Well, let's do a bit of tweaking in this task.

```
gem_wrap 'gem_persistence' => 'persistence.jar' do |t|
    project_path = Dir.pwd
    (1..2).each { project_path = File.dirname(project_path)}
    t.project = File.basename(project_path)
    t.version = '1.0'
end
```

Perfect! We have a nice gem that has been generated for us. And now what? Well, to be able to reference that gem as a dependency, it must be installed in your local gem repository, right? So RubyGems should help us here. The following command will do just what we want:

```
gem install target/coconut-persistence-1.0.gem
```

Now the module is available as a standard gem. That's pretty simple. Well, it could be easier actually. You know already when building the project that you want to have that gem installed, so calling RubyGems seems to be a step that could be made automatic. After all, that's what Raven is all about: being lazy with your build so you can spend your time doing more interesting stuff.

There's another task that includes this last installation step: gem_wrap_inst. It works like gem_wrap, but additionally, it does the installation automatically after generating the gem. Our example therefore becomes this:

```
gem_wrap_inst 'gem_persistence' => 'persistence.jar' do |t|
    t.version = '1.0'
end
```

Now that the module has been installed as a local gem, just like any other gem would, it's time for other modules to use it. In our example, the business module uses the gem produced by the persistence module. So we declare this dependency in the rakefile of the business module:

```
dependency 'module-deps' { |t| t.deps << 'coconut-persistence' }
```

Then we just need to declare this task as a prerequisite for any other task that relies on the persistence project, and it will work:

```
javac 'compile' => 'module-deps'
```

A Full Project Build

Being able to reuse another module is pretty nice, but that doesn't make a real multimodule build. You'll quickly see that there's a lack of synergy and reuse in the builds of these modules, as you can't trigger a global build with just one command, for example. So we're going to continue with the simple coconut web application example and go one step further with it. We won't use anything specific to Raven in this section; it's going to be just Rake and Ruby. It's also a good way for me to show you the strength of Raven's building blocks.

You might be thinking that the coconut example is too simple. However, even with only three modules, we can cover a lot of ground and use all the techniques you've learned so far. After working through this example, you should be able to find solutions to most of your build problems.

You've already seen all the pieces that would constitute the build scripts for the coconut project, but I haven't shown you a full script yet. So here is the rakefile for the persistence module:

```
require 'raven'
javac 'persistence.compile'
jar 'persistence.jar' => 'persistence.compile'
gem_wrap_inst('persistence.gem' => 'persistence.jar') { |t| t.version = '1.0' }
```

Yes, it has only four lines—so much condensed in so few characters just for your enjoyment. And everything should be pretty straightforward in these lines, as you've already seen all the tasks. The script compiles, builds a JAR, and builds and installs a gem.

Note ➡ Keep in mind that these tasks can be configured to fit most build and directory structures. Here, we're just sticking with the default directory structures.

Now let's see the rakefile for the business module:

```
require 'raven'
dependency 'business.deps' do |t|
    t.deps << 'coconut-persistence'
end
javac 'business.compile' => 'business.deps'
jar 'business.jar' => 'business.compile'
gem_wrap_inst('business.gem' => 'business.jar') { |t| t.version = '1.0' }
```

The rakefile for the web module looks nearly the same. Only the task names change, and the dependency is on the business module, instead of the persistence module. And beside the dependency declaration, the scripts for the persistence and business modules are similar as well.

TRYING IT OUT WITH IRB OR JIRB

Often when you're developing small scripts in Ruby, you want to try things out and see how they execute. Creating a Ruby script file and executing it with a Ruby or JRuby interpreter is a bit of overkill when you just want to experiment. Fortunately, Ruby has a command-line interpreter that allows you to easily run everything. It's called irb, for Interactive RuBy. JRuby also has its own version, called jirb.

Feel free to keep an open irb (or jirb) session on the side. Whenever you're not sure about what something does exactly or you just want to experiment, simply type in the commands! For example, you might try a script this way:

```
%> irb
irb(main):001:0> def add(a,b)
irb(main):002:1>   a + b
irb(main):003:1> end
=> nil
irb(main):004:0> add(3,2)
=> 5
irb(main):005:0> add('beautiful ', 'world')
=> "beautiful world"
```

If you're a browser person or if you happen to not have a Ruby interpreter installed on your machine yet, there's a very nice site that does exactly the same thing as irb, but online: http://tryruby.hobix.com/.

A Common Rakefile to Eliminate Redundancy

Our first improvement will be to get rid of all this unnecessary redundancy. We still want to define the tasks necessary to build the modules somewhere, but we don't want to repeat them over and over. To achieve this goal, the natural way seems to be the introduction of a common script that could be included in each module script.

Extracting redundant parts of the previous scripts to create a common rakefile is pretty easy:

```
require 'raven'

def define_targets(module_name)
   javac "#{module_name}.compile" => "#{module_name}.deps"
   jar "#{module_name}.jar" => "#{module_name}.compile" do
      puts "Module in jar #{module_name}"
   end
   gem_wrap_inst("#{module_name}.gem" => "#{module_name}.jar") do |t|
      t.version = '1.0'
   end
end
```

This file would sit in the root directory of the project (directly in the coconut directory) and could be named common.rb, for example.

As you can see, the hard-coded module name has been replaced by a variable. However, the notation could seem a bit weird with those # symbols all over the place. They are actually just simple Ruby notation.

Using #{} inside a double quoted string allows you to include variable values directly in the string body. Here is a small example of execution from an irb session:

```
irb> 3.times { |count| puts "I have #{count} stones in my pocket." }
```

```
I have 0 stones in my pocket.
I have 1 stones in my pocket.
I have 2 stones in my pocket.
```

It's a pretty neat way to mix strings and variable values.

So let's see how our scripts for the persistence, business, and web modules look now. Here is the one for the persistence module (coconut/persistence/rakefile):

```
require 'raven'
require '../common.rb'

dependency 'persistence.deps'

define_targets('persistence')
```

The one for the business module (coconut/business/rakefile) looks like this:

```
require 'raven'
require '../common'

dependency 'business.deps' do |t|
    t.deps << 'coconut-persistence'
end

define_targets('business')
```

And finally, here's the script for the web module (coconut/web/rakefile):

```
require 'raven'
require '../common'

dependency 'web.deps' do |t|
    t.deps << 'coconut-business'
end

define_targets('web')
```

We've eliminated all redundancy. Each script is defining only its own module name and its dependencies, and then loading the common script. When this common script is loaded, you will end up with the following tasks being defined for each module:

- In the persistence module, persistence.compile, persistence.jar, and persistence.gem

- In the business module, business.compile, business.jar, and business.gem

- In the web module, web.compile, web.jar, and web.gem

If you wanted to compile, create a JAR, create a gem, and install this gem for your three modules, you would just need to type the following commands:

```
cd persistence
rake persistence.gem
cd ..
cd business
rake business.gem
cd ..
cd web
rake web.gem
```

Simple isn't it? Actually, it could be even easier than that, as you'll see in the next section.

Using a common build script has made our build much more powerful. Adding a task in it (any kind of task—a simple Rake task or any of Raven's tasks) makes it available for all modules. Repetition has been reduced, while still allowing the option to define a specific task in a single module. When your build gets more complex, you could even use several specialized common scripts, including some only in the module scripts that need them. In short, it's all pretty nifty.

One Task to Bind Them All

Now that we have proper scripts in all the modules with appropriate tasks, it would be nice if we could call them all in just one task execution. The preceding list of commands seems to be a lot of work. You need to go into each directory and execute the appropriate task with Rake. For now, we have only three modules, but just imagine a project with ten or twenty modules! A simple build could require quite a lot of typing.

We're going to create a real rakefile in the project root directory: coconut. This rakefile will contain all the tasks used to execute module tasks. Let's see this file's content.

```
MODULES = ['persistence', 'business', 'web']
task 'build' do
   MODULES.each do |m|
     puts "### Building #{m}"
     Dir.chdir(m) do
        load 'rakefile'
        Rake::Task["#{m}.gem"].invoke
     end
   end
end
```

Only a few lines are required, but there's a lot of Ruby here. Let's go over it so that you can fully understand what this file is doing.

The first thing to notice is that something is missing. Raven is not required here. We're using a simple task definition—the most basic Rake task that doesn't do anything special except what you tell it to do.

The script first defines the list of modules to build. But why did I use MODULES instead of modules? Just for the pleasure of it? Not quite. In Ruby, variable names starting with an uppercase letter are considered as constants, and if you try to redefine a constant value, the Ruby interpreter will issue a warning. This way, if someone tries to update the module list, you will know about it.

Then comes the definition of the task itself, named (very originally) build. The each method is an iteration method available for all arrays in Ruby. It loops over the provided block of code, passing each element of the array in the variable defined between pipe symbols (|). That's the |m| part. So within the code block, m will successively take each value contained in the MODULES array.

The puts command just writes the name of the module that is going to be built.

Dir.chdir(m) changes the current directory to the provided value—here, the directory for each module we iterate on. The nice thing about this method is that it accepts a code block, and the directory change will be effective only for that block. When the end of the block is reached, the original directory is restored.

GOOD VERSION NUMBERS

You will occasionally find projects using all kind of versioning policies. You may see a version "number" like 4.0.5-GA, 0.5-dev-2, or an even more creative one. A good version number should be both easy to understand by a human and easily parsable by a computer, to be able to compute version orders, for example.

The RubyGems project has therefore defined a "rational" versioning policy that you should try to follow. Here's a summary of the rules:

- Versions should be represented by three integers, separated by periods (for example, 1.2.3). The first integer is the major version number, the second is the minor version number, and the third is the build number.

- A change in the implementation detail should increment the build number.

- A change that doesn't break compatibility with earlier versions should increment the minor version number and reset the build number.

- An incompatible change (like a public API modification) should increment the major build number and reset the minor and build numbers.

- Any public release should have a different version number, which usually means incrementing the build number. So developers can continue to generate builds themselves without changing the version, but as soon as they make a public release, the version should be updated.

For more information about the rational versioning policy, check the RubyGems documentation at http://docs.rubygems.org/read/chapter/7.

And we've finally reached the most interesting part of the script. Within a module directory, we're loading its rakefile, which means that all the task definitions for that module will be loaded. Once all the module tasks are available, one of them can be directly called—here, the module-specific gem task. Rake gives us a nice way to retrieve task definitions from their names using Rake::Task[*taskname*]. This gives us a Rake task object, and calling the invoke method on it will trigger the task execution. So these lines are explicitly calling a Rake task, forcing its execution.

To sum up, we've defined a new build task within the root rakefile. It iterates on all the modules, loads their respective rakefile, and executes their gem installation task. After the whole execution, we have a full project build.

Let's see what the output looks like:

```
%> rake build
```

```
### Building persistence
Building path src/main/java
javac -classpath "target/classes" -sourcepath "src/main/java"
        -d target/classes src/main/java/p/*.java
Module in jar persistence
Built jar file persistence.jar.
Wrapping jar in a Gem
  Successfully built RubyGem
  Name: coconut-persistence
  Version: 1.0
  File: coconut-persistence-1.0-java.gem
### Building business
Using local gem coconut-persistence (1.0) to satisfy dependency coconut-persistence
Building path src/main/java
javac -classpath "~/.raven/gems/coconut-persistence-1.0-java/ext/persistence.jar
        :target/classes" -sourcepath "src/main/java"
        -d target/classes src/main/java/b/*.java
Module in jar business
Built jar file business.jar.
Wrapping jar in a Gem
  Successfully built RubyGem
  Name: coconut-business
  Version: 1.0
  File: coconut-business-1.0-java.gem
```

```
### Building web
Using local gem coconut-business (1.0) to satisfy dependency coconut-business
Building path src/main/java
javac -classpath "~/.raven/gems/coconut-business-1.0-java/ext/business.jar
        :target/classes" -sourcepath "src/main/java"
        -d target/classes src/main/java/w/*.java
Module in jar web
Built jar file web.jar.
Wrapping jar in a Gem
  Successfully built RubyGem
  Name: coconut-web
  Version: 1.0
  File: coconut-web-1.0-java.gem
```

An important point is that we want our build to be done in the right order. For example, the web module wouldn't compile if the business module hadn't been compiled beforehand. It's your responsibility to make sure that the MODULES array in the root rakefile is ordered in the correct way. Other tools just let you define dependencies between modules and then compute the build order. But in the end, it's the same: you need to give the basic dependency information. Generalizing the build task to anything of your liking shouldn't be hard now that you understand the principle of iterating on modules and calling their tasks, since it's only more of the same. Here, we're iterating on all our modules, but you could also imagine tasks working on a subset, building only certain modules, for example. This base gives you a lot of flexibility.

Cleanup

So far, we've been generating all kinds of nice things: compiled classes, JARs, gems, and all those fancy artifacts. Creation is always the most enjoyable part, but sooner or later, cleanup becomes necessary.

Cleanup is handled nicely by Rake. You just need to require the right thing and define what to clean exactly. Adding the following in the root rakefile of our coconut project will enable a global cleanup at the root level:

```
require 'rake/clean'
CLEAN = Dir.glob('*/target')
```

The call to require will define the clean task automatically. When called, this task will use the CLEAN constant value to see what to delete. Here, we're setting the value using Dir.glob(), which gives us a list of target folders located in each module.

Calling the tasks is the last step to eliminate all the dust:

```
%> rake clean
```

After this easy trick, it's time to get back to dependencies. The coconut project is ambitious, but it won't go far without any external libraries. We will want to manipulate XML, access databases, use a web framework, and so on. The easy way would simply be to declare the dependencies for each module in its respective rakefile. Just add a dependency task for external gems and add it as a prerequisite for other tasks. But obviously, there will be some overlap. And everyone hates having to define the same thing too many times.

The solution should be pretty obvious to you, acute reader. Just define dependencies or groups of reusable dependencies in the common script located in the project root. For example, for a Spring-based project, you could do this:

```
dependency 'spring.deps' do |t|
    t.deps << ['spring-context', 'spring-beans', 'spring-aop']
    ....
end
```

Then you would just need to add spring_deps as a prerequisite in each module using Spring in its respective dependency task, and you would be set! Recall that a dependency task can be declared as a prerequisite to another, as a way to group them. So you would end up with a module dependency declaration looking like this:

```
dependency 'persistence.deps' => ['spring.deps', 'hibernate.deps']
```

An alternative to this solution is also to declare variables that you can reuse in several dependency declarations. This way, you don't reuse the dependency task itself but rather its definitions.

```
spring_deps = ['spring-context', 'spring-beans', 'spring-aop']
dependency('spring.deps') { |t| t.deps << spring_deps }
```

This can also be mixed with the previous approach to compose your dependencies in an easily reusable manner. However, the preferred way is to rely mostly on dependency tasks.

As a rule of thumb, don't hesitate to create all the dependency declarations that suit your needs in common scripts that will then be loaded in the module's scripts. It's a good way to keep a tight control on all those dependencies that can quickly plague your project.

Summary

With this chapter, your feature set is complete. Oh yes, there's always the need for more, bigger, and better, but from here on, it's mostly going to be about integration with other tools. As far as Raven is concerned, you've learned everything you need to handle simple to complex builds.

You've seen the building blocks in the previous chapter. This chapter has been all about cementing these blocks together to build a strong house—as strong as the third little pig's house, to bar the wolf outside.

You've seen how to build a gem from your modules, how to install it, and how to use it in other modules. Most important, you've seen how to glue the build or isolated modules in a single coherent way, organize your dependencies, and call all your modules' builds in a single shot. Again, it's all pretty simple, but it's also powerful.

CHAPTER 5

Public or Private Repository

*The indispensable first step to getting the things you want out of life is this:
Decide what you want.*

Ben Stein

At the end of the previous chapter, I said that you had all the information you needed to use Raven, and that was true. However, you have one more choice to make: flexibility or control.

One option is to have all your external dependencies automatically installed for you. Raven has a public central repository with a lot of gems available at gems.rubyraven.org. So, you don't need to explicitly install project dependencies. Raven will just download them when they're first needed. It makes the startup much quicker when someone starts on a new project, or if you just want to build a project to see how it works.

On the other hand, you may want to have more control over the central repository you install from, or you may want to distribute your own libraries in a central repository. In this case, you can build your own repository. Raven extracts parts of Maven repositories and uses them to build a Java gem repository. And this new private repository can be used just by setting it in your rakefile, either replacing gems.rubyraven.org or keeping it. In keeping with the Raven philosophy, it's your choice.

Automatic Dependency Installation: The Grand Unified Repository

Having your dependencies automatically installed for you means that you do not need to explicitly execute raven install (as described in Chapter 3). It's a nice feature and a pleasant alternative to explicit installation using the Raven command line. Just be wary before jumping on the wagon. Sometimes by having things done for you, you surrender a bit of your control. However, with Raven you can always get back some control.

It's nice that Raven can get dependencies for you, but it can't get them out of thin air. Raven needs a source to download the gems from: a repository. For automatic installation, Raven uses a gem repository.

Raven has its own central repository that contains most existing Java libraries published as gems. There are more than 11,000 of them! The open source Java community is very prolific indeed. The repository is published at http://gems.rubyraven.org. You can go there and have a look. It contains the following files and directories:

- gems: A directory that contains all the gem files published by the repository. As I said, there are a lot of them, so be prepared for loading a *long* file list.

- quick: Another directory containing the compressed gem specifications for each published gem. RubyGems uses those to give you more information about a gem without having to download it completely.

- yaml: A file that contains the list of all published gem specifications formatted as YAML.

- yaml.Z: The compressed version of the yaml file (for quicker download).

Note ➡ If you've never heard of "YAML Ain't a Markup Language," you can visit the site of this serialization format at http://www.yaml.org/. It's commonly used in Ruby. YAML is quite simple, but understanding it isn't necessary to use either Raven or RubyGems.

The default configuration for Raven is to use this repository. So if you declare a dependency and Raven can't find it in your local repository, it will try to download it from there. Then it will ask RubyGems to install it in your local gem repository to make it available for all Raven tasks using the dependency mechanism.

Note ➡ If you want to see the content of a gem, that's quite simple. It's actually a tar file. This tar contains two files: the gemspec, compressed as a gzip, and the content, compressed as a tar.gz. So you can open these to see what's in the gem.

Keeping It Personal: Your Own Repository

Sometimes you just want to play it solo. Using the same central repository as everyone else is nice, but there are some valid reasons for wanting to have your own central repository, such as these:

- To save bandwidth by having all developers of your project pull dependencies from an internal server

- To publish the gems of your project for other internal projects to use

- To keep a tight control on the repository content

- To publish gems for non-open source projects you're using

Here, I'll explain how to set up your own central repository. Then you will just need to modify your rakefile slightly to tell Raven to get its gems from your central repository instead of the one located at gems.rubyraven.org.

FROM MAVEN TO RAVEN

For you, poor Maven 2 users, Raven has a special feature, just to make you feel warm and welcome to Raven. Instead of downloading all over again the libraries that you already have in your local Maven repository, Raven includes a migration tool. It sucks up all the content of the local Maven repository and installs gems for each found artifact. Run it once, and then you're set—no need to download anything more (at least for your current project).

To run the tool, just type this:

raven import

You will be asked a couple of questions, and then the migration will start. It's as simple as that!

And the nice thing about it is that you can still keep the central Raven repository and have your own private repository. So you could use your repository to pull gems for internal project gems and Raven's repository for all the open source libraries. See the section titled "From Your Own Libraries" for more details.

From a Maven Repository

The easiest way to build your central repository is by importing some of the libraries published in already existing (and numerous) Maven repositories. You can either import the whole repository or only a few artifacts. This is easy because there's a Raven command just for that.

To import the entire repository, run this command from the server you plan to use for your central repository:

%> raven repository

This will download all JARs and create gems in the current directory, under a gems subdirectory, for the whole content of the Maven repository (some companies do this to save bandwidth). When finished, it will generate all the indexes necessary for RubyGems to recognize this as a central repository.

To import specific libraries from the repository, just include them in the command (again, executed from the server you plan to use for your central repository). For example, to import just log4j, xerces, and xalan, use this command:

```
%> raven repository log4j xerces xalan
```

This variant allows you to provide a subset of the project libraries you want to import. It can save you a lot of time.

An important thing to note is that you can run raven repository several times. It will download only new things and will update the RubyGems indexes. So it's still quite efficient and allows you to do small additions and updates.

After you've imported the repository, run the following command:

```
%> raven server
```

This starts a web server in the current directory, serving the repository you've just built. To check it out, take a look at http://localhost:2233 and contemplate the published directory structure of your first gem repository (and if it's not the first, just try to remember the joy of your first time).

The server command is just a convenience. Your newly built central repository can actually be served by any web server. RubyGems will know what to do as long as you specify the URL to the repository root.

From Your Own Libraries

To publish your libraries in a gem repository, follow these steps:

1. Wrap your JAR in a gem.

2. Copy the generated gem in a specific directory.

3. Build the repository index.

Raven can't make this totally automatic because your JARs could come from various places, and it won't know how to classify them. When you build your project with Raven, gems are already generated for you. But if you get JARs from external locations, it requires a bit more work. So you'll have to handle that yourself using Ruby. But don't worry, you'll have some help. Raven already has some things that you can reuse, and I'll show you how this all works.

First, wrap your JAR in a gem. Here is an example of code that does just that:

```
require 'fileutils'
require 'rubygems'
require 'raven'

FileUtils.mkdir('ext') unless File.exist?('ext')
FileUtils.cp('/path/to/myjarfile-1.1.jar', 'ext')
artifact = Raven::Artifact.new('myproject', 'myjarname', '1.1', '')
gemspec = Raven.create_gemspec(artifact)
Gem::Builder.new(gemspec).build
```

It's really straightforward. You mostly have to know that Java gems are built by putting the JAR file itself in an ext subdirectory of the gem. That's why the script first creates this directory and copies the JAR in it. Then it's just instantiating an artifact that will contain the project, JAR, and version information, and finally build the gem. The result will be a gem named myproject-myjarname-1.1.gem.

The second step is just a copy operation, so there's nothing much to detail there.

Once you have all your gems ready, you'll need to make sure they're all stored in a directory named gem. Then from the parent of this directory, invoke this command:

```
require 'raven'
main_index([])
```

This will call the RubyGems index builder, and that generates all the necessary files. Once that step is finished, your repository is ready. You just have to start the web server that will serve all your gems:

```
%> raven server
```

Needless to say, all of this should be embedded in a nice Rake task in your project rakefile, just to make things even more simple.

The Direction to Your Repository

Now that your brand-new, beautiful repository is waiting for you to get some gems out of it, you will need to tell Raven about it. Just add the following in your rakefile:

```
set_sources(["http://localhost:2233"])
```

Yes, that's it. When the next dependency declaration is executed, Raven will automatically download the gems it can't find in your local repository.

Note ➡ The address here is localhost, as you'll probably test this first on your own machine. The final address should reflect the address of the server on which the repository will be published.

If you don't quite see how all of this fits together, here is a very simple yet complete example that sets the source, declares a dependency, and compiles using this dependency:

```
require 'raven'
set_sources(["http://myserver:2233"])
dependency "deps" do |t|
  t.deps << ['log4j-log4j']
end
javac "compile" => "deps"
```

Finally, to just add your own repository and keep the Raven central repository, replace the set_sources call with the following line:

```
sources << "http://myserver:2233"
```

Note that this can be called multiple times if you need to use several repositories. The repositories will be searched in the order you specified.

Summary

One of my teachers used to say that teaching is all about repetition—nailing hard each of your points so that people will remember them for not just a couple of days, but for all their lives. This book is far too short to exert that sort of influence on your brain, unless you plan to read it five or six times which, somehow, I doubt. Oh, you'll probably open it again a couple of times after having read these lines, just for reference. But that won't be a real reading, so it doesn't count. Still there are a few points that I'd like you to remember about Raven, hence the repetition.

Raven gives you choices and possibilities. It's a flexible tool that provides more than one way to achieve your goals. The path you take is yours to choose. I can give you some advice, which I've done in this book, but ultimately, you're the only one who knows your needs. And I trust you; you'll figure it out. Just remember that building a project is mostly a piece of cake.